A Woman's Garden of Prayer JOURNAL

BROADMAN & HOLMAN PUBLISHERS

Nashville, Tennessee

with words from

SARAH MADDOX & PATTI WEBB

Many Christian women are prayer warriors—great intercessors. Sometimes, however, they do not take the time to pray adequately for themselves. This journal focuses on praying for yourself as a Christian woman. It contains Scriptures and prayers dealing with various aspects of a woman's life.

How can you and I be the kind of women God desires us to be? How can we keep from conforming to the world's mold? Only as we spend much time alone in God's presence—as we come aside each day, setting our hearts on things above, seeking His face and His will.

God calls us to come into our prayer gardens to meet with Him there. He wants us to become intimate friends of His Son, Jesus Christ. In John 15:15 Jesus said, "I have called you friends." A friend is one in whom you can confide the deepest thoughts of your heart.

This daily time with the Lord is absolutely essential for our spiritual health. It is our lifeline to our Lord. Without it we will be powerless and unfruitful. But with it, we are ready to face the day, no matter what it may hold. For we can be assured that:

He will never leave us or forsake us. He will guide us and guard us.
He will give us the wisdom we need and the words we need.
He will give us courage and comfort. He will give us strength and a song to sing.
He will give us the joy of the Lord. His peace will surround us wherever we go.
He will hear and answer as we walk in the light of His presence.

Oh, let us spend much time in the garden of prayer. "My Savior awaits, and He opens the gates to the beautiful garden of prayer."

—*Sarah Maddox*

Pray continually.

This is the confidence we have in approaching God:
that if we ask anything according to his will, he hears us.

1 JOHN 5:14

PRAYER

Oh Lord, You have told us in Your Word that the prayer of the upright pleases You. I desire to be faithful in prayer, continually seeking Your face, never giving up. May I realize anew that with You, God, nothing is impossible; but without You, I can do nothing.

As I spend time each day in my prayer garden, I want to walk with You and talk with You. I want to experience the joy that comes from spending time in Your presence. Help me daily to draw near to You. As I go from this place, may I "walk in the light of your presence" all day long (Ps. 89:15b). In Jesus' precious name I pray, *amen*.

_____

_____

_____

_____

_____

_____

_____

_____

_____

_____

_____

_____

_____

_____

The prayer of the upright pleases him.

Then Jesus told his disciples . . .
that they should always pray and not give up.
LUKE 18:1

P R A Y E R

Oh my Father, how I do want my words to be pleasing to You today. Set a watch over my lips, so that I will know when to speak and when to remain silent. I pray that out of my mouth will flow words of wisdom and kindness. May my speech always be gracious, "seasoned with salt." May I know how to respond to each person I encounter. May I be slow to speak and slow to become angry. Help me to listen carefully to others, not interrupting their conversations. Prompt me to speak timely, fitting words. Thank You for helping me in this important area today. In Jesus' name, *amen*.

The lips of the righteous know what is fitting.

May the words of my mouth and the meditation of my heart be pleasing in your sight, O LORD, my Rock and my Redeemer.

PSALM 19:14

PRAYER

Dear God, thank You that Your divine power has given me every-thing I need to become a godly woman—a woman who pleases You. I praise You that as I believe and obey Your Word, I will become more like You. As I learn more about You, You will give me the power and knowledge to escape the corruption in the world caused by evil desires. In Your precious name, *amen*.

. . . you will fill me with joy
in your presence.

_____
_____
_____
_____
_____
_____
_____
_____
_____
_____
_____
_____
_____
_____
_____
_____
_____
_____

Get rid of all bitterness, rage and anger, brawling and slander,
along with every form of malice. Be kind and compassionate to one another,
forgiving each other, just as in Christ God forgave you.

EPHESIANS 4:26–27

PRAYER

Oh dear God, my soul waits upon You today. I know that my expectations are to be in You. I affirm that my sufficiency is from You and You alone. May I not attempt to live out this day in my own strength but in the strength which You supply. I praise You for Your love for me and Your faithfulness to me. As I now lay before You my requests, I will wait in expectation for Your answers. In Jesus' holy name, *amen*.

_____

_____

_____

_____

_____

_____

_____

_____

_____

_____

_____

_____

_____

_____

_____

_____

_____

_____

_____

_____

May the God of hope fill you with all joy and peace as you trust in him ...

*In the morning I lay my requests before you
and wait in expectation.*

PSALM 5:3B

Prayer

Lord Jesus, thank You for dying on the cross for my sins. By faith, I accepted You as my Savior and Lord. I praise You that I belong to You, and no one can ever snatch me out of Your hand.

It is my earnest desire to live a life of faith and obedience, overflowing with thanksgiving for all You have done. May I let my "roots" grow down into You and draw up nourishment from You. In this way my faith will grow strong and vigorous in the truth I have been taught. In Jesus' name, *amen*.

_____

_____

_____

_____

_____

_____

_____

_____

_____

_____

_____

_____

_____

_____

_____

The LORD is my strength, and my song;
he has become my salvation.

As you received Christ Jesus as Lord,
continue to live in him, rooted and built up in him,
strengthened in the faith as you were taught,
and overflowing with thankfulness.

COLOSSIANS 2:6–7

PRAYER

Oh Father, everything around me seems to be changing—my body, my family, my world. How grateful I am that You, Lord, never change. Therefore, regardless of the changes that occur in my life, I know I can trust You to keep on taking care of me just as You have in the past. I thank You that You will generously provide all that I need. You will make all grace abound to me. Then I will have plenty for myself as well as for others. In Jesus' name, *amen*.

"I, the LORD, do not change."

The LORD is the everlasting God. . . .
He gives strength to the weary and increases the power of the weak. . . .
but those who hope in the LORD will renew their strength.

ISAIAH 40:28–29, 31

PRAYER

Oh Father, You have commanded us to go into all the world and present the gospel. You have asked us to pray for workers who will plant seeds for Your harvest. I know You have called me for this purpose also. Therefore, today I commit (anew or for the first time) to spreading the gospel. I ask that You open a door for me to proclaim Your message. I am willing to go wherever You send me. When that door opens, may I present the message of the gospel clearly. Help me to make certain that my speech is always gracious, seasoned with salt. I want to know how to answer each person I encounter. In Jesus' name, *amen*.

_____

_____

_____

_____

_____

_____

_____

_____

_____

_____

_____

_____

_____

_____

"Therefore go and make disciples of all nations . . ."

And pray for us, too, that God may open a door for our message, so that we may proclaim the mystery of Christ. . . . Be wise in the way you act toward outsiders; make the most of every opportunity.

COLOSSIANS 4:3, 5

PRAYER

Father, I am asking You to do a new thing in my life. I pray that as this new thing springs forth, I will know it has come from You. I am looking to You, oh Lord, to make a road in my wilderness and rivers in my desert. I desire for my life to be like a watered garden, and like a spring whose waters never fail. In Jesus' name, *amen*.

Pray continually.

_____
_____
_____
_____
_____
_____
_____
_____
_____
_____
_____
_____
_____
_____
_____
_____
_____
_____
_____
_____

This is the confidence we have in approaching God:
that if we ask anything according to his will, he hears us.

1 JOHN 5:14

PRAYER

Oh Lord, You have told us in Your Word that the prayer of the upright pleases You. I desire to be faithful in prayer, continually seeking Your face, never giving up. May I realize anew that with You, God, nothing is impossible; but without You, I can do nothing.

As I spend time each day in my prayer garden, I want to walk with You and talk with You. I want to experience the joy that comes from spending time in Your presence. Help me daily to draw near to You. As I go from this place, may I "walk in the light of your presence" all day long (Ps. 89:15b). In Jesus' precious name I pray, *amen*.

The prayer of the upright pleases him.

Then Jesus told his disciples . . .
that they should always pray and not give up.

LUKE 18:1

PRAYER

Oh my Father, how I do want my words to be pleasing to You today. Set a watch over my lips, so that I will know when to speak and when to remain silent. I pray that out of my mouth will flow words of wisdom and kindness. May my speech always be gracious, "seasoned with salt." May I know how to respond to each person I encounter. May I be slow to speak and slow to become angry. Help me to listen carefully to others, not interrupting their conversations. Prompt me to speak timely, fitting words. Thank You for helping me in this important area today. In Jesus' name, *amen*.

_____

_____

_____

_____

_____

_____

_____

_____

_____

_____

_____

_____

The lips of the righteous know what is fitting.

_____

_____

_____

_____

_____

_____

_____

_____

_____

_____

_____

_____

_____

_____

_____

_____

_____

_____

May the words of my mouth and the meditation of my heart
be pleasing in your sight, O LORD, my Rock and my Redeemer.

PSALM 19:14

PRAYER

Dear God, thank You that Your divine power has given me every-thing I need to become a godly woman—a woman who pleases You. I praise You that as I believe and obey Your Word, I will become more like You. As I learn more about You, You will give me the power and knowledge to escape the corruption in the world caused by evil desires. In Your precious name, *amen*.

. . . you will fill me with joy
in your presence.

Get rid of all bitterness, rage and anger, brawling and slander,
along with every form of malice. Be kind and compassionate to one another,
forgiving each other, just as in Christ God forgave you.

EPHESIANS 4:26–27

PRAYER

Oh dear God, my soul waits upon You today. I know that my expectations are to be in You. I affirm that my sufficiency is from You and You alone. May I not attempt to live out this day in my own strength but in the strength which You supply. I praise You for Your love for me and Your faithfulness to me. As I now lay before You my requests, I will wait in expectation for Your answers. In Jesus' holy name, *amen*.

_____

_____

_____

_____

_____

_____

_____

_____

_____

_____

_____

_____

_____

_____

_____

_____

_____

_____

May the God of hope fill you with all joy and peace as you trust in him . . .

In the morning I lay my requests before you and wait in expectation.

PSALM 5:3B

P R A Y E R

Lord Jesus, thank You for dying on the cross for my sins. By faith, I accepted You as my Savior and Lord. I praise You that I belong to You, and no one can ever snatch me out of Your hand.

It is my earnest desire to live a life of faith and obedience, overflowing with thanksgiving for all You have done. May I let my "roots" grow down into You and draw up nourishment from You. In this way my faith will grow strong and vigorous in the truth I have been taught. In Jesus' name, *amen*.

_____

_____

_____

_____

_____

_____

_____

_____

_____

_____

_____

_____

_____

_____

_____

The LORD is my strength, and my song;
he has become my salvation.

As you received Christ Jesus as Lord,
continue to live in him, rooted and built up in him,
strengthened in the faith as you were taught,
and overflowing with thankfulness.

COLOSSIANS 2:6–7

PRAYER

Oh Father, everything around me seems to be changing—my body, my family, my world. How grateful I am that You, Lord, never change. Therefore, regardless of the changes that occur in my life, I know I can trust You to keep on taking care of me just as You have in the past. I thank You that You will generously provide all that I need. You will make all grace abound to me. Then I will have plenty for myself as well as for others. In Jesus' name, *amen*.

"I, the LORD, do not change."

The LORD is the everlasting God....
He gives strength to the weary and increases the power of the weak....
but those who hope in the LORD will renew their strength.

ISAIAH 40:28–29, 31

Prayer

Oh Father, You have commanded us to go into all the world and present the gospel. You have asked us to pray for workers who will plant seeds for Your harvest. I know You have called me for this purpose also. Therefore, today I commit (anew or for the first time) to spreading the gospel. I ask that You open a door for me to proclaim Your message. I am willing to go wherever You send me. When that door opens, may I present the message of the gospel clearly. Help me to make certain that my speech is always gracious, seasoned with salt. I want to know how to answer each person I encounter. In Jesus' name, *amen*.

"Therefore go and make disciples of all nations . . ."

And pray for us, too, that God may open a door for our message,
so that we may proclaim the mystery of Christ. . . . Be wise in the way
you act toward outsiders; make the most of every opportunity.

Colossians 4:3, 5

PRAYER

Father, I am asking You to do a new thing in my life. I pray that as this new thing springs forth, I will know it has come from You. I am looking to You, oh Lord, to make a road in my wilderness and rivers in my desert. I desire for my life to be like a watered garden, and like a spring whose waters never fail. In Jesus' name, *amen*.

Pray continually.

This is the confidence we have in approaching God:
that if we ask anything according to his will, he hears us.

1 JOHN 5:14

PRAYER

Oh Lord, You have told us in Your Word that the prayer of the upright pleases You. I desire to be faithful in prayer, continually seeking Your face, never giving up. May I realize anew that with You, God, nothing is impossible; but without You, I can do nothing.

As I spend time each day in my prayer garden, I want to walk with You and talk with You. I want to experience the joy that comes from spending time in Your presence. Help me daily to draw near to You. As I go from this place, may I "walk in the light of your presence" all day long (Ps. 89:15b). In Jesus' precious name I pray, *amen*.

The prayer of the upright pleases him.

Then Jesus told his disciples . . .
that they should always pray and not give up.

LUKE 18:1

PRAYER

Oh my Father, how I do want my words to be pleasing to You today. Set a watch over my lips, so that I will know when to speak and when to remain silent. I pray that out of my mouth will flow words of wisdom and kindness. May my speech always be gracious, "seasoned with salt." May I know how to respond to each person I encounter. May I be slow to speak and slow to become angry. Help me to listen carefully to others, not interrupting their conversations. Prompt me to speak timely, fitting words. Thank You for helping me in this important area today. In Jesus' name, *amen*.

The lips of the righteous know what is fitting.

May the words of my mouth and the meditation of my heart be pleasing in your sight, O LORD, my Rock and my Redeemer.

PSALM 19:14

PRAYER

Dear God, thank You that Your divine power has given me every-thing I need to become a godly woman—a woman who pleases You. I praise You that as I believe and obey Your Word, I will become more like You. As I learn more about You, You will give me the power and knowledge to escape the corruption in the world caused by evil desires. In Your precious name, *amen.*

_____

_____

_____

_____

_____

_____

_____

_____

_____

_____

_____

_____

_____

_____

_____

_____

_____

_____

*. . . you will fill me with joy
in your presence.*

_____
_____
_____
_____
_____
_____
_____
_____
_____
_____
_____
_____
_____
_____
_____
_____
_____
_____
_____

*Get rid of all bitterness, rage and anger, brawling and slander,
along with every form of malice. Be kind and compassionate to one another,
forgiving each other, just as in Christ God forgave you.*

EPHESIANS 4:26–27

PRAYER

Oh dear God, my soul waits upon You today. I know that my expectations are to be in You. I affirm that my sufficiency is from You and You alone. May I not attempt to live out this day in my own strength but in the strength which You supply. I praise You for Your love for me and Your faithfulness to me. As I now lay before You my requests, I will wait in expectation for Your answers. In Jesus' holy name, *amen*.

May the God of hope fill you with all joy and peace as you trust in him . . .

In the morning I lay my requests before you and wait in expectation.

PSALM 5:3B

Prayer

Lord Jesus, thank You for dying on the cross for my sins. By faith, I accepted You as my Savior and Lord. I praise You that I belong to You, and no one can ever snatch me out of Your hand.

It is my earnest desire to live a life of faith and obedience, overflowing with thanksgiving for all You have done. May I let my "roots" grow down into You and draw up nourishment from You. In this way my faith will grow strong and vigorous in the truth I have been taught. In Jesus' name, *amen*.

_____

_____

_____

_____

_____

_____

_____

_____

_____

_____

_____

_____

_____

_____

The LORD is my strength, and my song; he has become my salvation.

As you received Christ Jesus as Lord,
continue to live in him, rooted and built up in him,
strengthened in the faith as you were taught,
and overflowing with thankfulness.

COLOSSIANS 2:6–7

PRAYER

Oh Father, everything around me seems to be changing—my body, my family, my world. How grateful I am that You, Lord, never change. Therefore, regardless of the changes that occur in my life, I know I can trust You to keep on taking care of me just as You have in the past. I thank You that You will generously provide all that I need. You will make all grace abound to me. Then I will have plenty for myself as well as for others. In Jesus' name, *amen*.

"I, the LORD, do not change."

The LORD is the everlasting God. . . .
He gives strength to the weary and increases the power of the weak. . . .
but those who hope in the LORD will renew their strength.

ISAIAH 40:28–29, 31

PRAYER

Oh Father, You have commanded us to go into all the world and present the gospel. You have asked us to pray for workers who will plant seeds for Your harvest. I know You have called me for this purpose also. Therefore, today I commit (anew or for the first time) to spreading the gospel. I ask that You open a door for me to proclaim Your message. I am willing to go wherever You send me. When that door opens, may I present the message of the gospel clearly. Help me to make certain that my speech is always gracious, seasoned with salt. I want to know how to answer each person I encounter. In Jesus' name, *amen*.

"Therefore go and make disciples of all nations . . ."

_____
_____
_____
_____
_____
_____
_____
_____
_____
_____
_____
_____
_____
_____
_____
_____
_____
_____
_____

And pray for us, too, that God may open a door for our message,
so that we may proclaim the mystery of Christ. . . . Be wise in the way
you act toward outsiders; make the most of every opportunity.

COLOSSIANS 4:3, 5

PRAYER

Father, I am asking You to do a new thing in my life. I pray that as this new thing springs forth, I will know it has come from You. I am looking to You, oh Lord, to make a road in my wilderness and rivers in my desert. I desire for my life to be like a watered garden, and like a spring whose waters never fail. In Jesus' name, *amen*.

Pray continually.

This is the confidence we have in approaching God:
that if we ask anything according to his will, he hears us.

<small>1 JOHN 5:14</small>

P R A Y E R

Oh Lord, You have told us in Your Word that the prayer of the upright pleases You. I desire to be faithful in prayer, continually seeking Your face, never giving up. May I realize anew that with You, God, nothing is impossible; but without You, I can do nothing.

As I spend time each day in my prayer garden, I want to walk with You and talk with You. I want to experience the joy that comes from spending time in Your presence. Help me daily to draw near to You. As I go from this place, may I "walk in the light of your presence" all day long (Ps. 89:15b). In Jesus' precious name I pray, *amen*.

The prayer of the upright pleases him.

Then Jesus told his disciples . . .
that they should always pray and not give up.

LUKE 18:1

PRAYER

Oh my Father, how I do want my words to be pleasing to You today. Set a watch over my lips, so that I will know when to speak and when to remain silent. I pray that out of my mouth will flow words of wisdom and kindness. May my speech always be gracious, "seasoned with salt." May I know how to respond to each person I encounter. May I be slow to speak and slow to become angry. Help me to listen carefully to others, not interrupting their conversations. Prompt me to speak timely, fitting words. Thank You for helping me in this important area today. In Jesus' name, *amen.*

The lips of the righteous
know what is fitting.

May the words of my mouth and the meditation of my heart
be pleasing in your sight, O LORD, my Rock and my Redeemer.

PSALM 19:14

PRAYER

Dear God, thank You that Your divine power has given me every-thing I need to become a godly woman—a woman who pleases You. I praise You that as I believe and obey Your Word, I will become more like You. As I learn more about You, You will give me the power and knowledge to escape the corruption in the world caused by evil desires. In Your precious name, *amen*.

_____

_____

_____

_____

_____

_____

_____

_____

_____

_____

_____

_____

_____

_____

_____

_____

_____

. . . you will fill me with joy in your presence.

Get rid of all bitterness, rage and anger, brawling and slander,
along with every form of malice. Be kind and compassionate to one another,
forgiving each other, just as in Christ God forgave you.

EPHESIANS 4:26–27

PRAYER

Oh dear God, my soul waits upon You today. I know that my expectations are to be in You. I affirm that my sufficiency is from You and You alone. May I not attempt to live out this day in my own strength but in the strength which You supply. I praise You for Your love for me and Your faithfulness to me. As I now lay before You my requests, I will wait in expectation for Your answers. In Jesus' holy name, *amen*.

_____

_____

_____

_____

_____

_____

_____

_____

_____

_____

_____

_____

_____

_____

_____

_____

*May the God of hope fill you with all
joy and peace as you trust in him . . .*

In the morning I lay my requests before you
and wait in expectation.

PSALM 5:3B

PRAYER

Lord Jesus, thank You for dying on the cross for my sins. By faith, I accepted You as my Savior and Lord. I praise You that I belong to You, and no one can ever snatch me out of Your hand.

It is my earnest desire to live a life of faith and obedience, overflowing with thanksgiving for all You have done. May I let my "roots" grow down into You and draw up nourishment from You. In this way my faith will grow strong and vigorous in the truth I have been taught. In Jesus' name, *amen*.

The LORD is my strength, and my song; he has become my salvation.

As you received Christ Jesus as Lord,
continue to live in him, rooted and built up in him,
strengthened in the faith as you were taught,
and overflowing with thankfulness.

COLOSSIANS 2:6–7

PRAYER

Oh Father, everything around me seems to be changing—my body, my family, my world. How grateful I am that You, Lord, never change. Therefore, regardless of the changes that occur in my life, I know I can trust You to keep on taking care of me just as You have in the past. I thank You that You will generously provide all that I need. You will make all grace abound to me. Then I will have plenty for myself as well as for others. In Jesus' name, *amen*.

"I, the LORD, do not change."

_____

_____

_____

_____

_____

_____

_____

_____

_____

_____

_____

_____

_____

_____

_____

_____

_____

_____

_____

_____

_____

_____

_____

The LORD is the everlasting God. . . .
He gives strength to the weary and increases the power of the weak. . . .
but those who hope in the LORD will renew their strength.

ISAIAH 40:28–29, 31

PRAYER

Oh Father, You have commanded us to go into all the world and present the gospel. You have asked us to pray for workers who will plant seeds for Your harvest. I know You have called me for this purpose also. Therefore, today I commit (anew or for the first time) to spreading the gospel. I ask that You open a door for me to proclaim Your message. I am willing to go wherever You send me. When that door opens, may I present the message of the gospel clearly. Help me to make certain that my speech is always gracious, seasoned with salt. I want to know how to answer each person I encounter. In Jesus' name, *amen*.

"Therefore go and make disciples of all nations . . ."

And pray for us, too, that God may open a door for our message,
so that we may proclaim the mystery of Christ. . . . Be wise in the way
you act toward outsiders; make the most of every opportunity.

COLOSSIANS 4:3, 5

PRAYER

Father, I am asking You to do a new thing in my life. I pray that as this new thing springs forth, I will know it has come from You. I am looking to You, oh Lord, to make a road in my wilderness and rivers in my desert. I desire for my life to be like a watered garden, and like a spring whose waters never fail. In Jesus' name, *amen*.

Pray continually.

This is the confidence we have in approaching God:
that if we ask anything according to his will, he hears us.

1 JOHN 5:14

P R A Y E R

Oh Lord, You have told us in Your Word that the prayer of the upright pleases You. I desire to be faithful in prayer, continually seeking Your face, never giving up. May I realize anew that with You, God, nothing is impossible; but without You, I can do nothing.

As I spend time each day in my prayer garden, I want to walk with You and talk with You. I want to experience the joy that comes from spending time in Your presence. Help me daily to draw near to You. As I go from this place, may I "walk in the light of your presence" all day long (Ps. 89:15b). In Jesus' precious name I pray, *amen*.

_____

_____

_____

_____

_____

_____

_____

_____

_____

_____

_____

_____

_____

The prayer of the upright pleases him.

Then Jesus told his disciples . . .
that they should always pray and not give up.

LUKE 18:1

PRAYER

Oh my Father, how I do want my words to be pleasing to You today. Set a watch over my lips, so that I will know when to speak and when to remain silent. I pray that out of my mouth will flow words of wisdom and kindness. May my speech always be gracious, "seasoned with salt." May I know how to respond to each person I encounter. May I be slow to speak and slow to become angry. Help me to listen carefully to others, not interrupting their conversations. Prompt me to speak timely, fitting words. Thank You for helping me in this important area today. In Jesus' name, *amen.*

_____

_____

_____

_____

_____

_____

_____

_____

_____

_____

_____

_____

_____

_____

The lips of the righteous know what is fitting.

May the words of my mouth and the meditation of my heart
be pleasing in your sight, O LORD, my Rock and my Redeemer.

PSALM 19:14

PRAYER

Dear God, thank You that Your divine power has given me every-thing I need to become a godly woman—a woman who pleases You. I praise You that as I believe and obey Your Word, I will become more like You. As I learn more about You, You will give me the power and knowledge to escape the corruption in the world caused by evil desires. In Your precious name, *amen*.

_____

_____

_____

_____

_____

_____

_____

_____

_____

_____

_____

_____

_____

_____

_____

_____

*. . . you will fill me with joy
in your presence.*

Get rid of all bitterness, rage and anger, brawling and slander,
along with every form of malice. Be kind and compassionate to one another,
forgiving each other, just as in Christ God forgave you.

EPHESIANS 4:26–27

PRAYER

Oh dear God, my soul waits upon You today. I know that my expectations are to be in You. I affirm that my sufficiency is from You and You alone. May I not attempt to live out this day in my own strength but in the strength which You supply. I praise You for Your love for me and Your faithfulness to me. As I now lay before You my requests, I will wait in expectation for Your answers. In Jesus' holy name, *amen*.

_____

_____

_____

_____

_____

_____

_____

_____

_____

_____

_____

_____

_____

_____

_____

_____

_____

_____

_____

May the God of hope fill you with all joy and peace as you trust in him . . .

In the morning I lay my requests before you and wait in expectation.

PSALM 5:3B

PRAYER

Lord Jesus, thank You for dying on the cross for my sins. By faith, I accepted You as my Savior and Lord. I praise You that I belong to You, and no one can ever snatch me out of Your hand.

It is my earnest desire to live a life of faith and obedience, overflowing with thanksgiving for all You have done. May I let my "roots" grow down into You and draw up nourishment from You. In this way my faith will grow strong and vigorous in the truth I have been taught. In Jesus' name, *amen*.

The LORD is my strength, and my song;
he has become my salvation.

As you received Christ Jesus as Lord,
continue to live in him, rooted and built up in him,
strengthened in the faith as you were taught,
and overflowing with thankfulness.

COLOSSIANS 2:6-7

PRAYER

Oh Father, everything around me seems to be changing—my body, my family, my world. How grateful I am that You, Lord, never change. Therefore, regardless of the changes that occur in my life, I know I can trust You to keep on taking care of me just as You have in the past. I thank You that You will generously provide all that I need. You will make all grace abound to me. Then I will have plenty for myself as well as for others. In Jesus' name, *amen*.

_____

_____

_____

_____

_____

_____

_____

_____

_____

_____

_____

_____

_____

_____

_____

_____

_____

_____

"I, the LORD, do not change."

The LORD is the everlasting God. . . .
He gives strength to the weary and increases the power of the weak. . . .
but those who hope in the LORD will renew their strength.

ISAIAH 40:28–29, 31

PRAYER

Oh Father, You have commanded us to go into all the world and present the gospel. You have asked us to pray for workers who will plant seeds for Your harvest. I know You have called me for this purpose also. Therefore, today I commit (anew or for the first time) to spreading the gospel. I ask that You open a door for me to proclaim Your message. I am willing to go wherever You send me. When that door opens, may I present the message of the gospel clearly. Help me to make certain that my speech is always gracious, seasoned with salt. I want to know how to answer each person I encounter. In Jesus' name, *amen*.

"Therefore go and make disciples of all nations . . ."

And pray for us, too, that God may open a door for our message,
so that we may proclaim the mystery of Christ. . . . Be wise in the way
you act toward outsiders; make the most of every opportunity.

COLOSSIANS 4:3, 5

PRAYER

Father, I am asking You to do a new thing in my life. I pray that as this new thing springs forth, I will know it has come from You. I am looking to You, oh Lord, to make a road in my wilderness and rivers in my desert. I desire for my life to be like a watered garden, and like a spring whose waters never fail. In Jesus' name, *amen*.

Pray continually.

_This is the confidence we have in approaching God:
that if we ask anything according to his will, he hears us._

1 JOHN 5:14

PRAYER

Oh Lord, You have told us in Your Word that the prayer of the upright pleases You. I desire to be faithful in prayer, continually seeking Your face, never giving up. May I realize anew that with You, God, nothing is impossible; but without You, I can do nothing.

As I spend time each day in my prayer garden, I want to walk with You and talk with You. I want to experience the joy that comes from spending time in Your presence. Help me daily to draw near to You. As I go from this place, may I "walk in the light of your presence" all day long (Ps. 89:15b). In Jesus' precious name I pray, *amen*.

The prayer of the upright pleases him.

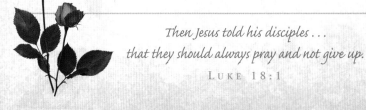

Then Jesus told his disciples . . .
that they should always pray and not give up.

LUKE 18:1

PRAYER

Oh my Father, how I do want my words to be pleasing to You today. Set a watch over my lips, so that I will know when to speak and when to remain silent. I pray that out of my mouth will flow words of wisdom and kindness. May my speech always be gracious, "seasoned with salt." May I know how to respond to each person I encounter. May I be slow to speak and slow to become angry. Help me to listen carefully to others, not interrupting their conversations. Prompt me to speak timely, fitting words. Thank You for helping me in this important area today. In Jesus' name, *amen.*

_____

_____

_____

_____

_____

_____

_____

_____

_____

_____

_____

_____

_____

_The lips of the righteous
know what is fitting._

_May the words of my mouth and the meditation of my heart
be pleasing in your sight, O LORD, my Rock and my Redeemer._

PSALM 19:14

PRAYER

Dear God, thank You that Your divine power has given me every-thing I need to become a godly woman—a woman who pleases You. I praise You that as I believe and obey Your Word, I will become more like You. As I learn more about You, You will give me the power and knowledge to escape the corruption in the world caused by evil desires. In Your precious name, *amen*.

_____

_____

_____

_____

_____

_____

_____

_____

_____

_____

_____

_____

_____

_____

_____

_____

_____

. . . you will fill me with joy
in your presence.

Get rid of all bitterness, rage and anger, brawling and slander,
along with every form of malice. Be kind and compassionate to one another,
forgiving each other, just as in Christ God forgave you.

EPHESIANS 4:26–27

PRAYER

Oh dear God, my soul waits upon You today. I know that my expectations are to be in You. I affirm that my sufficiency is from You and You alone. May I not attempt to live out this day in my own strength but in the strength which You supply. I praise You for Your love for me and Your faithfulness to me. As I now lay before You my requests, I will wait in expectation for Your answers. In Jesus' holy name, *amen*.

_____

_____

_____

_____

_____

_____

_____

_____

_____

_____

_____

_____

_____

_____

_____

_____

_____

May the God of hope fill you with all joy and peace as you trust in him . . .

In the morning I lay my requests before you and wait in expectation.

PSALM 5:3B

PRAYER

Lord Jesus, thank You for dying on the cross for my sins. By faith, I accepted You as my Savior and Lord. I praise You that I belong to You, and no one can ever snatch me out of Your hand.

It is my earnest desire to live a life of faith and obedience, overflowing with thanksgiving for all You have done. May I let my "roots" grow down into You and draw up nourishment from You. In this way my faith will grow strong and vigorous in the truth I have been taught. In Jesus' name, *amen*.

_____

_____

_____

_____

_____

_____

_____

_____

_____

_____

_____

_____

_____

_____

_____

_____

_____

The LORD is my strength, and my song; he has become my salvation.

As you received Christ Jesus as Lord,
continue to live in him, rooted and built up in him,
strengthened in the faith as you were taught,
and overflowing with thankfulness.

COLOSSIANS 2:6–7

PRAYER

Oh Father, everything around me seems to be changing—my body, my family, my world. How grateful I am that You, Lord, never change. Therefore, regardless of the changes that occur in my life, I know I can trust You to keep on taking care of me just as You have in the past. I thank You that You will generously provide all that I need. You will make all grace abound to me. Then I will have plenty for myself as well as for others. In Jesus' name, *amen*.

_____

_____

_____

_____

_____

_____

_____

_____

_____

_____

_____

_____

_____

_____

_____

_____

_____

_____

_____

"I, the LORD, do not change."

The LORD is the everlasting God....
He gives strength to the weary and increases the power of the weak....
but those who hope in the LORD will renew their strength.

ISAIAH 40:28–29, 31

PRAYER

Oh Father, You have commanded us to go into all the world and present the gospel. You have asked us to pray for workers who will plant seeds for Your harvest. I know You have called me for this purpose also. Therefore, today I commit (anew or for the first time) to spreading the gospel. I ask that You open a door for me to proclaim Your message. I am willing to go wherever You send me. When that door opens, may I present the message of the gospel clearly. Help me to make certain that my speech is always gracious, seasoned with salt. I want to know how to answer each person I encounter. In Jesus' name, *amen*.

"Therefore go and make disciples of all nations ..."

And pray for us, too, that God may open a door for our message,
so that we may proclaim the mystery of Christ. . . . Be wise in the way
you act toward outsiders; make the most of every opportunity.

COLOSSIANS 4:3, 5

PRAYER

Father, I am asking You to do a new thing in my life. I pray that as this new thing springs forth, I will know it has come from You. I am looking to You, oh Lord, to make a road in my wilderness and rivers in my desert. I desire for my life to be like a watered garden, and like a spring whose waters never fail. In Jesus' name, *amen*.

Pray continually.

This is the confidence we have in approaching God:
that if we ask anything according to his will, he hears us.

1 JOHN 5:14

PRAYER

Oh Lord, You have told us in Your Word that the prayer of the upright pleases You. I desire to be faithful in prayer, continually seeking Your face, never giving up. May I realize anew that with You, God, nothing is impossible; but without You, I can do nothing.

As I spend time each day in my prayer garden, I want to walk with You and talk with You. I want to experience the joy that comes from spending time in Your presence. Help me daily to draw near to You. As I go from this place, may I "walk in the light of your presence" all day long (Ps. 89:15b). In Jesus' precious name I pray, *amen*.

The prayer of the upright pleases him.

Then Jesus told his disciples . . .
that they should always pray and not give up.

LUKE 18:1

PRAYER

Oh my Father, how I do want my words to be pleasing to You today. Set a watch over my lips, so that I will know when to speak and when to remain silent. I pray that out of my mouth will flow words of wisdom and kindness. May my speech always be gracious, "seasoned with salt." May I know how to respond to each person I encounter. May I be slow to speak and slow to become angry. Help me to listen carefully to others, not interrupting their conversations. Prompt me to speak timely, fitting words. Thank You for helping me in this important area today. In Jesus' name, *amen*.

_____

_____

_____

_____

_____

_____

_____

_____

_____

_____

_____

_____

_____

_____

_____

The lips of the righteous know what is fitting.

May the words of my mouth and the meditation of my heart be pleasing in your sight, O LORD, my Rock and my Redeemer.

PSALM 19:14

PRAYER

Dear God, thank You that Your divine power has given me everything I need to become a godly woman—a woman who pleases You. I praise You that as I believe and obey Your Word, I will become more like You. As I learn more about You, You will give me the power and knowledge to escape the corruption in the world caused by evil desires. In Your precious name, *amen*.

_____

_____

_____

_____

_____

_____

_____

_____

_____

_____

_____

_____

_____

_____

_____

_____

_____

. . . you will fill me with joy in your presence.

PRAYER

Oh dear God, my soul waits upon You today. I know that my expectations are to be in You. I affirm that my sufficiency is from You and You alone. May I not attempt to live out this day in my own strength but in the strength which You supply. I praise You for Your love for me and Your faithfulness to me. As I now lay before You my requests, I will wait in expectation for Your answers. In Jesus' holy name, *amen*.

_____

_____

_____

_____

_____

_____

_____

_____

_____

_____

_____

_____

_____

_____

_____

_____

_____

May the God of hope fill you with all joy and peace as you trust in him . . .

In the morning I lay my requests before you and wait in expectation.

PSALM 5:3B

Prayer

Lord Jesus, thank You for dying on the cross for my sins. By faith, I accepted You as my Savior and Lord. I praise You that I belong to You, and no one can ever snatch me out of Your hand.

It is my earnest desire to live a life of faith and obedience, overflowing with thanksgiving for all You have done. May I let my "roots" grow down into You and draw up nourishment from You. In this way my faith will grow strong and vigorous in the truth I have been taught. In Jesus' name, *amen*.

_____

_____

_____

_____

_____

_____

_____

_____

_____

_____

_____

_____

_____

_____

The LORD is my strength, and my song; he has become my salvation.

As you received Christ Jesus as Lord,
continue to live in him, rooted and built up in him,
strengthened in the faith as you were taught,
and overflowing with thankfulness.

COLOSSIANS 2:6–7

PRAYER

Oh Father, everything around me seems to be changing— my body, my family, my world. How grateful I am that You, Lord, never change. Therefore, regardless of the changes that occur in my life, I know I can trust You to keep on taking care of me just as You have in the past. I thank You that You will generously provide all that I need. You will make all grace abound to me. Then I will have plenty for myself as well as for others. In Jesus' name, *amen*.

"I, the LORD, do not change."

The LORD is the everlasting God. . . .
He gives strength to the weary and increases the power of the weak. . . .
but those who hope in the LORD will renew their strength.

ISAIAH 40:28–29, 31

Prayer

Oh Father, You have commanded us to go into all the world and present the gospel. You have asked us to pray for workers who will plant seeds for Your harvest. I know You have called me for this purpose also. Therefore, today I commit (anew or for the first time) to spreading the gospel. I ask that You open a door for me to proclaim Your message. I am willing to go wherever You send me. When that door opens, may I present the message of the gospel clearly. Help me to make certain that my speech is always gracious, seasoned with salt. I want to know how to answer each person I encounter. In Jesus' name, *amen*.

"Therefore go and make disciples
of all nations . . ."

And pray for us, too, that God may open a door for our message,
so that we may proclaim the mystery of Christ. . . . Be wise in the way
you act toward outsiders; make the most of every opportunity.

COLOSSIANS 4:3, 5

PRAYER

Father, I am asking You to do a new thing in my life. I pray that as this new thing springs forth, I will know it has come from You. I am looking to You, oh Lord, to make a road in my wilderness and rivers in my desert. I desire for my life to be like a watered garden, and like a spring whose waters never fail. In Jesus' name, *amen*.

Pray continually.

This is the confidence we have in approaching God:
that if we ask anything according to his will, he hears us.

1 JOHN 5:14

Prayer

Oh Lord, You have told us in Your Word that the prayer of the upright pleases You. I desire to be faithful in prayer, continually seeking Your face, never giving up. May I realize anew that with You, God, nothing is impossible; but without You, I can do nothing.

As I spend time each day in my prayer garden, I want to walk with You and talk with You. I want to experience the joy that comes from spending time in Your presence. Help me daily to draw near to You. As I go from this place, may I "walk in the light of your presence" all day long (Ps. 89:15b). In Jesus' precious name I pray, *amen.*

The prayer of the upright pleases him.

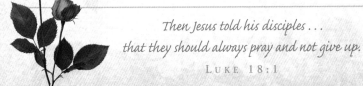

Then Jesus told his disciples . . .
that they should always pray and not give up.

LUKE 18:1

PRAYER

Oh my Father, how I do want my words to be pleasing to You today. Set a watch over my lips, so that I will know when to speak and when to remain silent. I pray that out of my mouth will flow words of wisdom and kindness. May my speech always be gracious, "seasoned with salt." May I know how to respond to each person I encounter. May I be slow to speak and slow to become angry. Help me to listen carefully to others, not interrupting their conversations. Prompt me to speak timely, fitting words. Thank You for helping me in this important area today. In Jesus' name, *amen*.

_____

_____

_____

_____

_____

_____

_____

_____

_____

_____

_____

_____

_____

*The lips of the righteous
know what is fitting.*

*May the words of my mouth and the meditation of my heart
be pleasing in your sight, O LORD, my Rock and my Redeemer.*

PSALM 19:14

PRAYER

Dear God, thank You that Your divine power has given me everything I need to become a godly woman—a woman who pleases You. I praise You that as I believe and obey Your Word, I will become more like You. As I learn more about You, You will give me the power and knowledge to escape the corruption in the world caused by evil desires. In Your precious name, *amen*.

_____

_____

_____

_____

_____

_____

_____

_____

_____

_____

_____

_____

_____

_____

_____

_____

_____

_____

*. . . you will fill me with joy
in your presence.*

Get rid of all bitterness, rage and anger, brawling and slander,
along with every form of malice. Be kind and compassionate to one another,
forgiving each other, just as in Christ God forgave you.

EPHESIANS 4:26–27

PRAYER

Oh dear God, my soul waits upon You today. I know that my expectations are to be in You. I affirm that my sufficiency is from You and You alone. May I not attempt to live out this day in my own strength but in the strength which You supply. I praise You for Your love for me and Your faithfulness to me. As I now lay before You my requests, I will wait in expectation for Your answers. In Jesus' holy name, *amen*.

May the God of hope fill you with all joy and peace as you trust in him . . .

In the morning I lay my requests before you and wait in expectation.

PRAYER

Lord Jesus, thank You for dying on the cross for my sins. By faith, I accepted You as my Savior and Lord. I praise You that I belong to You, and no one can ever snatch me out of Your hand.

It is my earnest desire to live a life of faith and obedience, overflowing with thanksgiving for all You have done. May I let my "roots" grow down into You and draw up nourishment from You. In this way my faith will grow strong and vigorous in the truth I have been taught. In Jesus' name, *amen*.

The LORD is my strength, and my song;
he has become my salvation.

As you received Christ Jesus as Lord,
continue to live in him, rooted and built up in him,
strengthened in the faith as you were taught,
and overflowing with thankfulness.

COLOSSIANS 2:6–7

PRAYER

Oh Father, everything around me seems to be changing—my body, my family, my world. How grateful I am that You, Lord, never change. Therefore, regardless of the changes that occur in my life, I know I can trust You to keep on taking care of me just as You have in the past. I thank You that You will generously provide all that I need. You will make all grace abound to me. Then I will have plenty for myself as well as for others. In Jesus' name, *amen.*

"I, the LORD, do not change."

The LORD is the everlasting God....
He gives strength to the weary and increases the power of the weak....
but those who hope in the LORD will renew their strength.

ISAIAH 40:28–29, 31

Prayer

Oh Father, You have commanded us to go into all the world and present the gospel. You have asked us to pray for workers who will plant seeds for Your harvest. I know You have called me for this purpose also. Therefore, today I commit (anew or for the first time) to spreading the gospel. I ask that You open a door for me to proclaim Your message. I am willing to go wherever You send me. When that door opens, may I present the message of the gospel clearly. Help me to make certain that my speech is always gracious, seasoned with salt. I want to know how to answer each person I encounter. In Jesus' name, *amen.*

"Therefore go and make disciples of all nations . . ."

And pray for us, too, that God may open a door for our message,
so that we may proclaim the mystery of Christ. . . . Be wise in the way
you act toward outsiders; make the most of every opportunity.

COLOSSIANS 4:3, 5

PRAYER

Father, I am asking You to do a new thing in my life. I pray that as this new thing springs forth, I will know it has come from You. I am looking to You, oh Lord, to make a road in my wilderness and rivers in my desert. I desire for my life to be like a watered garden, and like a spring whose waters never fail. In Jesus' name, *amen*.

You will be like a well-watered garden,
like a spring whose waters never fail.

Praise be to the God and Father
of our Lord Jesus Christ!
In his great mercy he has given
us new birth into a living hope
through the resurrection of
Jesus Christ from the dead.

1 PETER 1:3

In the Garden

I come to the garden alone,

While the dew is still on the roses;

And the voice I hear,

falling on my ear,

The Son of God discloses.

And He walks with me, and He talks with me

And He tells me I am His own,

And the joy we share as we tarry there,

None other has ever known.

—*C. Austin Miles*